About the Author

Kamalaathmika Sarangan is an eight-year-old, Tamil, Sri Lankan girl. Having been born in Sri Lanka, she is now a British Citizen and lives in Milton Keynes, England, with her parents. She adores birds, and her passion has led her to write fifty poems about a variety of different birds. When she was three years old, she wrote her first poem, 'The Condors'. Kamalaathmika has a vast knowledge of ornithology, and aspires to be an ornithologist one day. To have her poems published is a dream come true for Kamalaathmika.

She is extremely creative, and excels at art and creative writing. She learns the piano, as well as South Indian Carnatic music – she composes music too. Furthermore, she performs academic studies exceptionally well.

Kamalaathmika's family hail from Nainativu, or Manipallavam, an island of historical importance off the Jaffna peninsula.

50 Bird Poems

Kamalaathmika Sarangan

50 Bird Poems

Olympia Publishers
London

www.olympiapublishers.com
OLYMPIA PAPERBACK EDITION

Copyright © Kamalaathmika Sarangan 2022

The right of Kamalaathmika Sarangan to be identified as author of this work has been asserted in accordance with sections 77 and 78 of the Copyright, Designs and Patents Act 1988.

A CIP catalogue record for this title is available from the British Library.

ISBN: 978-1-80074-698-5

This is a work of fiction.
Names, characters, places and incidents originate from the writer's imagination. Any resemblance to actual persons, living or dead, is purely coincidental.

First Published in 2022

Olympia Publishers
Tallis House
2 Tallis Street
London
EC4Y 0AB

Printed in Great Britain

Dedication

I dedicate this book to my parents, grandparents, uncles, aunties, cousins, teachers and the little birds who inspired me.

Acknowledgements

Thank you to the little birds who inspired me to write this
book.

The Snow Bunting

Snow Bunting, Snow Bunting, white as snow,

The fluffy snow fellow, that you know.

He's cute, and small, with snow-white feathers,

He has a flock, that flocks like heathers.

He's very light, and always jumping,

The little bird, the white Snow Bunting.

The Ostrich

From all of the sights that I see down brown lanes,

Bushes and houses, and even white planes!

Each time I see one, I run faster and faster,

Racing my friends, and calling out 'Laster!'

Go past the meadows and look out for bees,

Go past the butterflies and the tall trees.

Go past the waterhole, lions and kings,

Go past the gold giraffe, and wriggly things.

Racing the leaves as they fall to the ground,

Hopping and skipping and running around.

Watching my friends going at a slow pace,

I cross the finish line, and win the race!

The Greater Bird of Paradise

Red, like the sunset skies,

Blue, like sweet lullabies.

The Greater Bird of Paradise,

Is on his way to Heaven.

Dancing sweetly, every day,

Singing to me, on the way,

My favourite bird, that is today,

With his friends, all seven.

The pretty bird has joined a flock,

That flies around the world-wide clock,

He pecked a watch, it went tick-tock,

With his flock now eleven.

I went home, and crossed my heart,

Then I sat, and ate a tart,

I dreamt with pleasure, in my cart,

Thinking of lovely Keven.

The Blue Tit

I am the very, fluffy bird,

The one that sits and flits,

I like to eat organic curd,

And like to do the splits.

I am quite blue, I'm *azure* blue,

With a light-yellow breast,

I have a thing that's a strange hue,

The black line on my chest.

I like to sit, in tall, tall, trees,

That grow in garden bits,

I am the one, that always flees,

The azure blue, blue tit.

The Magpie and the moon

Once upon a time,
A long time ago,
There once lived a young magpie,
And her name was Tago.

She was wandering around,
And looking at a loon,
Until she saw some white,
A sliver of the moon.

"Tago, Miss Tago,
What brings you out so late?
Aren't you supposed to be in bed,
Behind the leafy gate?"

"I know it feels wrong,
Yes, all of it is true,
But what lies beyond the leafy gate,
Is something that's not blue!"

"Oh that's the sky, not to lie,
Now you know, that is why,
So quickly fly off into bed,
Before you're a lost magpie!"

Robin, robin

Robin, Robin, up in the treetops, can you hear me call?

The tree you're in is so, so, high and also very tall!

My feathered friend, aren't you afraid, for I fear you may fall!

Robin, Robin, up in the treetops, can you hear me call?

Ode to a Nuthatch

Oh Nuthatch, I kindly praise you,
Oh Nuthatch, make me fly too!

Oh Nuthatch, look at your beautiful, blue crest,
Oh Nuthatch, look at your wonderful, red breast!

Oh Nuthatch, stay in the tree,
Oh Nuthatch, please don't flee!

Oh Nuthatch, all so blue,
Oh Nuthatch, this can't be true!

Oh Nuthatch, my feathered friend,
Make sure your glory may never end.

The Parrot

"Hello", "Hello"

"Fellow", "Fellow"

"Yellow", "Yellow"

The Parrot copies what I say.

"Green", "Green"

"Preen", "Preen"

"Clean", "Clean"

The Parrot does this every day.

"Red", "Red"

"Head", "Head"

"Tread", "Tread"

Well done sweet Parrot, that's the way!

"Macaw", "Macaw"

"Touca", "Touca"

"Carrot", "Carrot"

Good girl, soft Parrot.

The Chaffinch

Oh you sweet downy, cute red bird,

Who flies above a working herd,

 And this is what I tend to say,

Today's the day, it's Wednesday!

Today's the day, that you were born,

The time, when I first fed you corn,

You smiled a very big bright smile,

Which made my joyed heart leap a mile.

You made my day, the times I cried,

I tried to guess, I tried, I tried,

You'd chirp, and give me a small pinch,

You lovely bird, you peach Chaffinch.

The Flamingo

I'm pink, and have a long, long neck,

My name is Miss Flamingo,

Would you have guessed that is my name?

Well, if you did, then BINGO!

I eat red substance, called algae,

That only grows in water,

It's delicious, makes me think,

I have to feed my daughter!

The Red Kite

The ferocious Red Kite,

He always knows what's right.

He catches other birds,

Up to crow or gull size,

And eats them so quickly,

Before I blink my eyes.

He makes high-drawn wailing,

And that is his voice,

He makes high-pitched squealing,

That gives him a choice.

As I told you before,

He always knows what's right,

The very so bright,

The handsome Red Kite.

The Indian Peacock

I know I'm a Peacock,
Just look at my feathers,
They are so pretty,
Just like mauve heathers.

I cannot fly,
Very well at all,
If I touch the sky,
I may quickly fall.

I eat berries and shrubs,
Small seeds, and green grubs,
I'm turquoise, purple, and blue,
Yes, all of it is true.

I am the bird, that is best,
The bird best than rest.

I'm proud about that,
You know where I'm at.

Describe me with all the best words,
For I'm better than the other old birds.

Even better than an old rock,
The so proud bird, the jade Peacock.

The Pomarine Skua

I really do wonder why,

Pomarine Skuas can fly!

Because they're ever so big,

They'd certainly get in a jig!

They really don't need wings at all,

These feathers just soften the fall!

Now I know why they have wings,

Or they're not the one that sings…

But eating mussels and fish?

With wings tipped in beige, - brownish,

They fell in a bucket of cream,

And the green ground they did seam.

Stomping around with their feet,

The birds really dropped the beat.

These lovely birds, have the ways that are,

The best to be a Skua.

Oh, Young Chickadee

Oh, look at me, as I fly high,

Oh, look at me, as clouds go by!

Oh, look at me, young Chickadee,

Please come along, and fly with me!

Cold winter, summer, spring and fall,

That little tree, it's grown so tall!

Circling it would be fine by me,

What do you think, young Chickadee?

The House Sparrow

Chirping to a song,
In my birdhouse all day long.

At the bird feeder I eat,
Bird bath's where I keep neat.

I wake up at dawn,
When strange humans roll and yawn.

Water has to be clean,
Or I'll scoff, and say, "That's mean."

A garden filled with silver marrow?
Perfect for a small House Sparrow.

The Swallow

Chirrup, Chirrup, I go!

Chirrup, Chirrup, I go!

On my way back home!

On my way back home!

I'm a little Swallow, that goes Cheep, Cheep!

I'm a little Swallow, who goes Tweet, Tweet!

I'm a little Swallow, who likes to sing,

I'm a little Swallow, with lots of seeds to bring!

Chirrup, Chirrup, I go!

Chirrup, Chirrup, I go!

On my way back home!

On my way back home!

I'm a little Swallow, that goes Tweet, Tweet!

I'm a little Swallow, who goes Cheep, Cheep!

Winter's over, and it's nearly Spring,

Come along, and see what I bring!

The Owl

I hunt at night,
The moon's so bright!
I eat the mice I catch,
There're lots of birds, and fish, and bugs,
In the forest patch.

I cough up fur, and bones, and feathers,
In little balls, called pellets,
I also have some baby birds,
And they're named little owlets.

I hunt at night, and am nocturnal,
As I told you so,
Cos' my mousy prey is crawling down,
So I have to fly low.

I have to fly down, to the ground,
Spinning plant weed, all around.
And all the time, I watch the pond,
Looking carefully, all along.

And I get wet, so what's the matter?
I don't need a towel,
For I'm the very fearsome bird,
The very, strongly owl.

The Cuckoo

Cuckoo, Cuckoo, it makes a sound,
Cuckoo, Cuckoo, flying all around.

Cuckoo, Cuckoo, flying in the trees,
Cuckoo, Cuckoo, the Cuckoo flees.

Cuckoo, Cuckoo, eating corn,
Cuckoo, Cuckoo, wings all worn.

Cuckoo, Cuckoo, lays egg with warbler,
Cuckoo, Cuckoo, fights with shoveler.

Cuckoo, Cuckoo, on the cattle,
Cuckoo, Cuckoo, won a battle.

Cuckoo, Cuckoo, in the thunder,
Cuckoo, Cuckoo, hear dogs' blunder.

Cuckoo, Cuckoo, fly away,
Cuckoo, Cuckoo, come back again.

The Ruff

Oh, the very proudy Ruff,

Who shows off his splendid buff.

On his head, something like ears,

I think he uses them for steers.

He buffs his breast, as he crows,

"Which birds are ugly? Who knows?"

He's lots of pride, in his mind,

But that's common, for his kind.

Oh, you Ruff, the proud creature,

You have such a great feature!

But keep in mind, that pride's not cool,

Or you swim in swimming pool!

Remember, Ruff, I'm warning you,

Just give me a hug, you fuzzy two!

The Twelve-Wired-Bird-of-Paradise

Twelve Wired Bird of Paradise — ise — ise,

Oh, Twelve Wired Bird of Paradise — ise — ise,

Oh, did you eat all of my cooked rice — ice — ice?

Oh, Twelve Wired Bird of Paradise — ise.

The Long — Tailed — Tropicbird

Look at the seabird,
Look at the seabird,

Flying around in the air,

Huddling up,
Huddling up,

All round the great town square.

It's eating corn with lots of fish,
It is funny, that I wish.

Flying around, bumping into trees,
The Long — Tailed — Tropicbird always flees.

The Redstart

Redstart, Redstart, all so blue,
The sound you make is just a coo.

Redstart, Redstart, crimson is true,
Redstart, Redstart, tail long too.

Redstart, Redstart, on a branch,
Sitting peacefully, like in a trance.

Redstart, Redstart, in a tree,
Redstart, Redstart, please don't flee!

The Ring Ouzel

Oh, Ring Ouzel, neck so bright,

Glowing radiantly, throughout the night.

So one or another, another or one,

I hope the Ring Ouzel is just having fun.

Until the Ring Ouzel, in the evening flies away,

'Come back Ring Ouzel,' I may call and stay.

My Friendly Magpie

I love my friendly magpie,
She's very, very, cute,
I once asked her to make a noise,
She made a funny toot.

She's very, very, special,
And also very good,
That's why I give her breakfast,
With heaps, and heaps, of food.

Sometimes she gets upset,
And I know why is that,
'Cos very friendly magpies,
Do not like fat, grey cats.

She's my favourite magpie,
In all the Seven Seas,
And I love her very much,
I hope she too loves me.

The Inca Tern

Oh, wonderfully grand, Inca Tern.
Oh, wonderfully grand, Inca Tern.
Can I see, your wings?

Oh, beautiful one,
Oh, beautiful one,
Are you the one, that sings?

Your hue,
Your feathers, all slate-grey!
And scarlet puffin legs,

Your long, white beard,
With ends that teared!
Resembles silver pegs!

The Penguin

Blizzard, blizzard, setup wizard,

Where did the Penguin go?

Here and there, here and there,

And oh, is that the Penguin's toe?

Oh no it's not, it looks quite dull,

That's not the Penguin, it's the gull!

Oh, and Penguin swam away,

And then let out a loud squawk hull.

Oh there he is, found him at last,

This Penguin adventure was such a blast!

The Mute Swan

My neck is an S.

Uno, Dos, Tres.

I am all white,

Please don't fight.

My bill is orange,

My friend is Twan,

My feet are webbed,

I am the swan.

The Dove

I'm the dove,

I spread love.

I eat seeds,

Help birds' needs.

Christmas is here,

Let ducks to peer.

Spread lots of love,

And help the dove.

The Condors

Whenever I sit, under the famous oak tree,
I always see two condors, bouncing up and down in glee.
So when I call out to them, the lovebirds give a shriek!
'Squik — squak — songey!' they call back to me.

The Pitohui

I know very well,
Stay away from this bird,
It's described with poison,
Yes, that is the word.

Poisonous bugs,
Are what it does eat,
Poison travels to its feathers,
Which makes it bad, but sweet.

It follows red light,
On light buoy,
The troublesome bird,
The cute Pitohui.

The Greylag Goose

I live in a pond,

Surrounded in reeds,

It keeps me safe,

And gives all a goose needs.

It's very wet,

And I like swimming,

I migrate in winter,

And it's all worth a shilling.

I also moult in autumn,

And have chicks in the spring,

I am all brown;

And that's all a good thing.

I also have a little friend,

And he's the friendly moose,

He's big inside, and outside too,

And my name's Mrs.Goose.

The Hummingbirds

These American birds,

Are described with three words;

Fast, quick and brilliant,

I named one Jiliant.

My pet eats curd,

Oh, the wonderful hummingbird.

The Pink Robin

I have a pink breast,

And that is my chest.

I'm pink and black,

Black on my back.

I have a pet,

It was nice when we first met.

He's a ladybug,

His greatest friend was a chocolate pug.

I like to weave, and use a bobbin,

'Cos I'm the very rose-pink robin.

The Cirl Bunting

I am the yellow Cirl Bunting!

I'm very, very, tiny,

I like to sit in willow trees-

That always smell a bit piny.

I eat little insects,

But vegan except for that,

I have lots of predators;

Especially the tubby, grey cat.

I also have a weird friend,

One that's always out hunting,

Though he doesn't hunt me,

'Cos I'm the citrine Cirl Bunting.

The Wood Pigeon

I'm blue,

With a grey hue.

Yes, it is true,

That I am blue.

I know a widgeon,

For I'm the Pigeon.

And as I say,

Grey is my way,

So call me a Wood Pigeon.

The Mallard Duck

Pet a duck,

And get a buck.

I am all beige,

Specked with golden-brown,

My beak is amber,

And I have a brown crown.

My neck is white,

So fly a kite.

My oily feathers, I do tuck,

For I'm the ornate, Mallard Duck.

The Blackbird

I'm black, with a yellow beak,
And my feet, oh, they're thin and meek.

I forage around, scurrying for nuts,
Staring along, at saggy, brown huts.

I fly to gardens, with lots of seeds,
With my onyx eyes, that look like beads.

I like to fly, and go away,
But don't worry, I'll come back and stray.

The Female Crow

Watch the female Crow,
As you see her glow;
Picking berries away,
As she does this every day.

Watch the female Crow,
As you see her glow;
Picking berries, every day,
As she does this away.

You can see her glow;
By watching the female Crow.

The Starling

I am a galaxy,

With black feathers, that are swirly.

See me on a tree,

Don't come close, or I'll flee.

Pet a marlin, and get a Starling.

The Nightingale

I sing so sweetly,

Yet oh, quite weakly,

With brown feathers,

And green heathers.

Altogether, makes me better,

Alone in one dark night.

The days last long,

To hear my song,

Amidst the rainy thunder,

Lights all shine,

That gives me time,

To sing the noon away,

To hear cats blunder,

And to spend the day.

The Coal Tit

I'm a coal tit,

So let be it.

Over the bright blue sky,

Flying around is so much fun,

When you're chasing

The clouds up high.

I eat bugs,

Sit under rugs,

Under the sky so blue,

So let be it.

Things are much more fun,

When you're a coal tit too.

The Cardinal

Cardinal, oh Cardinal, oh Cardinal, so red.

Do you like, oh do you like, oh do you like your head?

Are you on, oh are you on, are you in your soft bed?

Cardinal, oh Cardinal, oh Cardinal so red.

The Bohemian Waxwing

A starling like passerine,
That breeds in North America,
A fluffy little waxwing,
That sits on plants called Erica.

Fuzzy, creamy wings,
With waxy tips,
A small, curved beak,
That looks like lemon pips.

Like a superhero,
In the night,
Your inky bib,
It glows so bright!

Oh, you,
Amazing Avifauna,
Now you perch on,
The lily; Amaryllis Belladonna.

So follow me now,
If you please,
Into my picture,
And say CHEESE!

Oh, you bird,
I need your max — sing,
You small, you bird,
You Bohemian Waxwing.

The Canary

Canary, Canary, all so yellow,

Canary, Canary, you little fellow.

Canary, Canary, a wonderful song,

Canary, Canary, golden tail so long.

Canary, Canary, eating cranberries,

Canary, Canary, pecking at cherries.

Canary, Canary, your notes are all slurred,

Canary, Canary, you're my favourite bird.

The Mountain Bluebird

Mountain Bluebird, Mountain Bluebird,
Your colour is so blue!
I bet your feathers are so shiny,
They attract your food.

A soft, silver-white underside,
And a sapphire body, that goes with the tide.
A mountainous habitat,
As you hop on a rabbit at,

An errand; just to find a seed,
To feed his family, and succeed.
Bluebird here would visit gardens and parks,
If it weren't for those horrendous barks,

Of dogs, who lost a frisbee or,
Of those, who search the trees for more.
Many dogs, such a lurcher,
Scare away this frightened percher.

Exhausted as the bird may seem,
He just likes to sit and beam.
So come into my garden to,
Eat the seeds I have for you.

Come on, just stay,
You have my word,
Just sing to me,
Mountain Bluebird.

The Mynah

Mynah, Mynah, flying so high,

Won't you take me up in the sky?

You have black feathers, and two wings,

A sooty chest, and gold eye rings.

You fly upon the great, grey wall,

I was just thinking, won't you fall?

You've coal-black feathers, all so great,

You bird, you're very hard to hate!

You sit up on a tree with height,

Don't you just even get a fright?

Oh, Mynah, please say yes, yes, yes,

That you're the bird that's best than rest!

I can't describe you with any word,

For you're better than another bird.

I think I'll name you little Pine Ah,

You inky bird, you lovely Mynah.

The Dunnock

Look at that! A bird in the sky;

Look at that! A Dunnock bird;

Look at that! A bird's flying high;

I can't describe it with any word.

Citrine tummy, and garnet back,

For winter, I don't want you to pack!

Do you want to eat seeds,

Or would rather a worm-

The light pink ones,

That dig and squirm?

I bet your barn friend's, a, fun cock,

You citrus, diamond, small Dunnock.

The Long-Tailed-Tit

I know this, you may have heard,

That I'm a very, long-tailed bird.

My tail is longer, than my body,

And that's what, I've meant to embody.

Listen here, listen from this avian,

Listen here, whose ancestors are pavian.

My tummy is, a colour called taffy,

My wings are edged in buff,

Some people tend, to think I'm daffy,

Including the proud old ruff.

I like to fly, above my nest,

And perch on oak trees, free to rest.

You may not see me, in seasons round the globe,

Especially not, in your wardrobe.

To bird feeders, I just go,

To eat the suet, I fly so slow.

To catch some bugs, I hatched a plan,

The burrowing owl, has dug a pit,

I guess this is just, much more than I can,

For I'm a cute, and brave, Long-Tailed-Tit.

The Rooster & the Moose

Cock-a-doodle-doo! Cock-a-doodle-doo!

Rooster, Rooster, I have worms for you!

Cock-a-doodle-doo!

He crows at dawn,

Cock-a-doodle-doo!

There goes a fawn!

Emerald, sapphire, onyx, and ruby too,

All of these colours, are worth a doodle-doo!

Oh no!

Here comes a moose!

Run away, or you'll get trampled,

Fly away, you silly goose!

The space is getting crampled!

Wow!

You get a leaf, and lure her away,

Twisting, and turning, round the barn all day!

Now the moose, is tired all good,

What a great way to out — moose her,

Now eat those worms now, if you could,

You sweet, you male, you Rooster.

The Hoatzin

This bird gives off such a strange odour,

Hoatzin, Hoatzin, learn a modor!

Eat all the bugs, that you want,

But to a blenny, don't you taunt.

Your pretty crest, that stands upright,

As you fly around, a stalactite.

Oh, you very, fuzzy, red Mordor,

Please just listen, to my order.

Beautiful sapphire, lush, emerald green,

You're not as naughty, as it may seem.

Whenever you want,

Send a post in,

Telling me that you need a visit,

You sweet Hoatzin.